Here's to the joyous sounds
and sweet smells of
Christmas!

This fartrageous book belongs to

_____

_____

Copyright © 2022 A Matter of Rhyme

All rights reserved. No part of this publication, or the characters within, may be reproduced or distributed in any form or by any means without prior written consent from the publisher.

ISBN 978-1-958741-00-9

Visit amatterofrhyme.com to see more children's books by the author.

THE TWELVE FARTrageous DAYS OF CHRISTMAS

By I.M. Witty

Illustrated by Daniel Wlodarski

Mrs. Claus settles in and begins to work. Hours pass, and her tummy starts to rumble. She closes her weary eyes and rests her head on the desk.

A short break won't hurt.

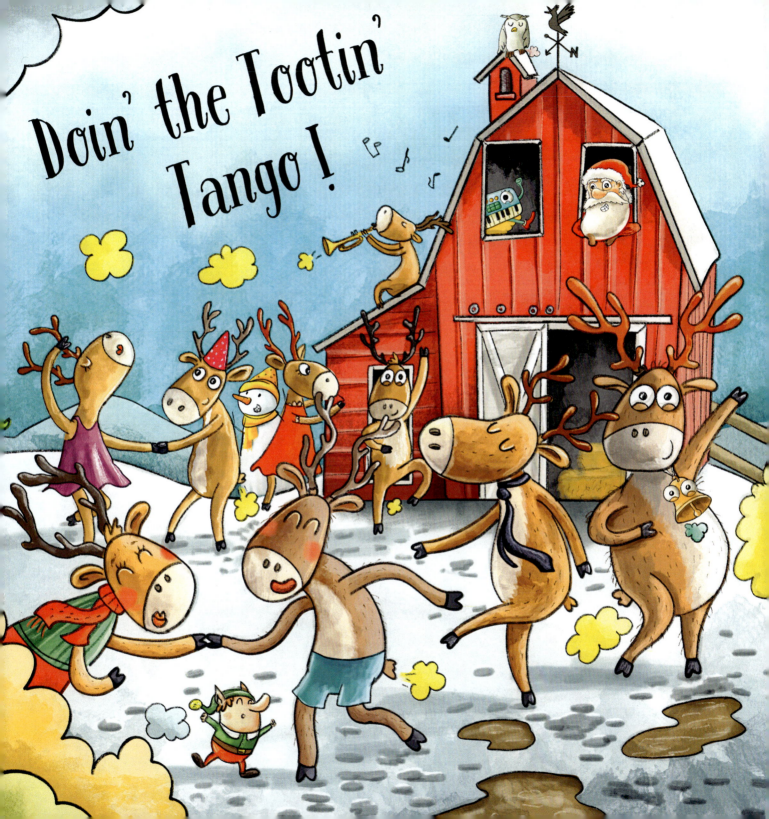

Fart Smarts

 Farting is the process of releasing gas from your bottom.

 Farts can seem sneaky, smelly, or silly, but it's important to know that everyone farts!

 Foods you eat and drink and how your body uses the food cause farting.

 There are many names for farts or farting: flatulence, poots, toots, bottom burps, breaking wind, passing gas – just to name a few.

 Most farts do not have an odor.

Healthy people can fart between 12 to 25 times in one day.

 Farts are estimated to travel 6.8 miles per hour.

 You cannot hold in a fart.

 Most farts happen at night while you sleep.

 While all people fart, some animals do not, such as sloths, birds, and certain sea creatures.

 If you fart around other people, use good manners and say, "Excuse me."

I.M. Witty (aka Sheri Wall) is a lover of rhyme who has lived in Texas for a really long time. She would read to her sons and kids that she knew, and they all enjoyed rhyming picture books too. Then A Matter of Rhyme began as a dream to help others learn with zippy rhyme schemes. Sheri likes to stay active and be on the go, either biking, shopping, or seeing a show. To find more lively books by this witty mom, visit her website amatterofrhyme.com

Daniel Wlodarski is a creator of children's book illustrations and covers and is an animation artist. He lives in a tree house with his wife, two sons, and a daughter. When he is not drawing, he is floating on a tire swing, dreaming about what clouds taste like, and holding his breath for a time. Visit Daniel's website, danielwlodarski.com.

Made in United States
North Haven, CT
20 November 2023